S0-AQC-525

Jokes, cartoons and quotes
from New Fjord, Minnesota

101
UFF
DAS

By Ed Fischer

Plus a 'cheer up' section for those
with too many uff das in their life

© Ed Fischer

For additional copies write
Ed Fischer, 57 Viking Village
Rochester, Minnesota 55901
or call 507 281-5119

ISBN 0-9624482-2-2

Dedicated to all Scandinavians,the
beautiful people with a wonderful sense
of humor, but especially to Lavonne.

Uff Da *(Oof dä) interj*
Scandinavian exclamation of surprise
or frustration as in: "You won the lottery but
you're disqualified because your brother-
in-law works for the lottery." Uff da!
Can also be used as an expression of
endearment and love as in "Congratulations,
you're the proud Papa of triplets...again."
Uff da!

A situation
where the
expression
uff da
may be used

ED FISCHER

On November 23, 1976, the meaning of "Uff da"
was sealed in a Minnesota Bicentennial Time Capsule
to be opened on July 4, 2075.
Here is some of what was put in that capsule...

**"Uff da" is an all-purpose expression covering
a variety of situations such as:**

UFF DA is...trying to dance the polka to rock and roll music.
UFF DA is...having a mouse crawl up your leg on a hay ride.
UFF DA is...waking yourself up in church with your own snoring.
UFF DA is...noticing non Norwegians using lefse for napkins
        at a church dinner.
UFF DA is...sneezing so hard that your false teeth end up in
        the punch bowl.
UFF DA is...not being Norwegian.

a little lunch

ED FISCHER

is today the day you cook lutefisk, Reverend?

First Lutheran

ED FISCHER

8

9

Leif taught his dog to play poker,
but he lost a fortune.
Every time the dog gets a good
hand, he wags his tail.

Leif's apartment was so cold, every time
he opened his door a light would go on.

Fern: "I'm famous for my tuna casserole
        and my apple strudel."
Leif: "Which one is this?"

The New Fjord Airlines is so cheap, instead
of movies the pilot shows slides of
his family.

The
early bird
wouldn't
get the
worm
if the worm
would
sleep late

– Fjlmar Tingleson
Norwegian philosopher

Uff da! Oscar and Ingrid were
happily married for
only a short time...

ED FISCHER

15

Leif found out the hard way the latch goes on the inside of the door

Leif rushed into a drugstore and says,
" Do you have something for hiccups?"
Without warning, the druggist hits him
in the face.
Leif yells,"What in thunder did you do
that for?"
"Well, you don't have the hiccups anymore,
do you?", the druggist says.
"No," says Leif," but my wife out in the car does."

At the New Fjord Hotel:

"Would you like a room with a tub
or a shower?"
"What's the difference?"
"With a tub you sit down."

The New Fjord Blue Ox Lounge
featured a topless lady ventriloquist.
Not one person saw her lips move.

Leif has a lot of trouble with his ticklish cow...

Ed Fischer

ATTENDANT ON DUTY

SHOE SHINE

ED FISCHER

Say-
lutefisk
would be a
welcome change

ED FISCHER

20

Maybe
you can't
hear
opportunity
knocking
because the
TV
is too
loud

-Fjlmar Tingleson
Norwegian Philosopher

ED FISCHER

Northlands Nudist Colony
MEDICAL ALERT

DO NOT attempt to play the accordian naked!

ED FISCHER

Einstein
never
had
a
VCR

– Fjlmar Tingleson
Norwegian Philosopher

New Fjord
Historical Site
FIRST AND LAST
MINNESOTA OUTHOUSE
BUILT ON A ROCK
BUILT   CLOSED
OCT. 1985   NOV. 1985

ED FISCHER

Leif had a pig who could sing the
Minnesota Rouser. Knowing how
unbelievable this was, he bet Oscar
fifty dollars that his pig could sing.
Oscar took the bet, but the pig was silent.
Oscar took Leif's money, laughed and left.
"What's the matter with you?", Leif
yelled at the pig,"Why didn't you sing?
You just cost me fifty dollars!"
"Cool your jets," said the pig,"Think
how much we'll take the sucker for
next time."

Leif has a new microwave TV set.
Now he can watch Sixty Minutes in
six minutes.

Oscar entered the Indy 500. He made
eighty pit stops...three for gas and
seventy-seven to ask directions.

Can you spit through that beard?

Why do you ask?

It's on fire.

Leif was out of town when Leona gave
birth to twins, a boy and a girl.
In the county where they lived, it was the
law that the babies were to be named
within two days..
Unable to get back, Leif reluctantly asked
his dimwit brother Oscar to help name the
babies.
Upon his return, Leif rushed to his wife,
fearing the worse. "Tell me quick," Leif
said, "What did you call the girl?"
"Denise", was her reply. "That's not
so bad", Leif said, "What did you call
the boy?" "De nephew."

If
at first
you don't
succeed,
your
skydiving
days are
over

— Fjlmar Tingleson
Norwegian philosopher

New Fjord
Blood
Bank

ED FISCHER

Oscar:

Can you lend me $50. until payday?

Leif:

When's payday?

Oscar:

How should I know? When do you get paid?

Fortunately, Leif designed his house with an emergency exit

*A few
more things
to do with
lutefisk...*

...a breakfast drink to
wake up with...

few people know that the planet Mars is made of lutefisk...

(...the scientific explanation of why there's no life there)

Leif went to a movie. The movie was so bad,
everyone was standing in line to get out.

Leif: "Oscar likes sports but today he played real bad.
     He even lost a ball."
Fern:"He shouldn't feel bad. Lots of people lose golf balls."
Leif: "Oscar was bowling."

Coffee can be bad for you. Leif knows someone
who went blind drinking coffee.
She kept leaving the spoon in the cup.

Leif went shopping. What a ritzy place! He asked
for something under fifty dollars, and they looked
in the garbage.

Oscar thinks maybe it's the food he eats that's keeping people away.

ED FISCHER

Only YOU can prevent lutefisk!

ED FISCHER

41

Leif couldn't afford to go to
Niagara Falls on his honeymoon,
so he drove through a car wash
real slow.

Sven was seventy-five and his
bride was twenty-one.Their honeymoon
lasted for 6 days and Sven didn't
leave her alone. Exausted, the girl left
to get a cup of coffee at a nearby cafe.
The waitress said, "I saw how old your
husband is, why do you look so awful?"
The bride said,"When he said he was saving
up for fifty years, I thought he meant money."

Leif read where drinking is bad for you.
So, he gave up reading.

Leif's efficiency
expert at work
saved the
company $600
a week.

He quit.

46

laugh
and the
world
laughs with
you—
snore and
you sleep
alone

— Fjlmar Tingleson
Norwegian philosopher

NEW FJORD
BOOKS

TODAY: ELVIS presley
Autobiography
Author book signing today

ED FISCHER

Sick?
take two
lutefisk
and call
me in the
morning!

51

make your own
weather indicator...

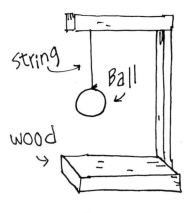

string →

Ball ↙

wood ↘

ED FISCHER

How to operate;

- If the ball is moving, it is windy.
- If the ball is wet, it is raining.
- If the ball is white, it is snowing.
- If the ball is gone, it is a tornado.

ED FISCHER

A magician and parrot were crossing the
ocean on a ship. The magician was performing
his tricks for the passengers when
a parrot in the back of the room yelled,
"Where's the tricks?" This upset the magician.
The next night he did his better tricks, but still
the parrot screeched, "Where's the tricks?"
This really rattled the magician, so the next night
he did his very best tricks, when the ship hit
a mine and blew up.
There were only two survivors, the magician
and parrot. Finally, the parrot looked at the
magician and said, "Okay, I admit it was
a good trick, what did you do with the ship?"

ED FISCHER

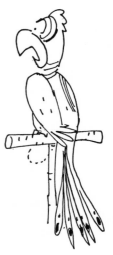

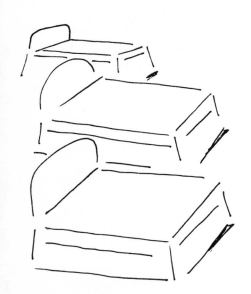

SALE USED WATER BEDS

ED FISCHER

are we 100% sure cats can't fly?

ED FISCHER

the pot at the end of the rainbow

ED FISCHER

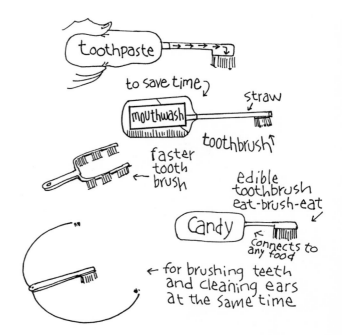

Ideas for a new, better toothbrush...

toothpaste

to save time

mouthwash — straw

toothbrush

faster tooth brush

edible toothbrush eat-brush-eat

Candy — connects to any food

← for brushing teeth and cleaning ears at the same time

Ingrid encounters the
first case of
sexual harassment
by a computer...

61

Too many uff das in your life?
Now is the time to...

Cheer Up

things could be worse...

MY SHIP'S COME IN—
MY SHIP'S COME IN...

TITANIC

ED FISCHER

Spice up
your
Conversation-
Quote
yourself...

If you
can't get
a
compliment
any other
way,
pay yourself
one

–Mark Twain

It is
better to
live rich
than to
die
rich

—Samual Johnson
1729-1784

Cheer-up activity

From your car yell..

Don't forget about tonight!

ED FISCH

The best way
to cheer yourself
up is to try to
cheer someone
else up

—Mark Twain

For example...

- Read the comics to a Kid.
- Leave a note to someone telling them how special they are.
- On no special occasion, send a greeting card or a page from this book to someone.
- Send flowers
- Serve your neighbors breakfast in bed (let them know first)
- Stop your car on the side of the road and give your wife or lover a kiss. (Not recommended for car pools)

Huggers
make
better
lovers

When you get worried,
and you can't sleep,
count your blessings
instead of sheep—
and you'll fall asleep
counting your blessings

—1950s song by
Eddie Fisher

ED FISCH

Think of everyday
as a gift...

ED FISCHER.

Other books by Ed Fischer...

"101 things to do with lutefisk" 4.95
"Minnesota: A cold love affair" $6.95
Add $2.00 shipping

Sweatshirts and T-shirts...

Multi-colored $18.95 sweatshirt, $12.95 T-shirt. Indicate gray or white S, M, L, XL plus $2.50 shipping

"What's so funny about getting old?" By Ed Fischer and Jane Nolan, CompCare Publishers $7.95
Add $2.00 shipping

Write Ed Fischer, 57 Viking Village, Rochester, Minnesota 55901 or call 507 281-5119

71

Other sweatshirts and T-shirts...

Multi-colored $18.95 sweatshirt, $12.95 T-shirt. Indicate gray or white S, M, L, XL plus $2.50 shipping

Every day
is a
gift

Screaming
uses up
120
calories

HUG
SQUAD

OFFICIAL HUGGER 1

Mugs...

HOW TO QUIT SMOKING...

Lutefisk filter

Lutefisk eaters make better lovers

lutefisk recipe'

lutefisk Surprise

1. Take one lutefisk
2. Get rid of it

UFF DA!

Merry Lutefisk

Lutefisk isn't just for breakfast anymore

72

$45.00 per dozen

$6.50 each plus $1.50 shipping